The Mountain Within You

Transforming Self-Sabotage into Self-Mastery Through Discipline, Courage, and Powerful Daily Habits

BY: Asharaf Ali

Copyright

ISBN: 978-93-5912-494-0

Published by A.A. Mind Growth Books

This book is intended for **educational and motivational purposes only**. While every effort has been made to ensure accuracy, the author makes no guarantees regarding specific results. Individual outcomes may vary based on personal effort, circumstances, and consistency. The reader is solely responsible for their own actions, decisions, and results.

Disclaimer

The content of this book is based on the author's personal insights, research, and observations. It does not constitute professional advice of any kind, including but not limited to medical, legal, financial, or psychological advice. Readers are encouraged to consult qualified professionals when appropriate.

Any references to real individuals, public figures, or real-life situations are used strictly for educational and motivational purposes. Such references are based on publicly available information, including interviews, biographies, and public records. The author does not claim any personal association, endorsement, or direct relationship with any individuals mentioned.

All opinions expressed are solely those of the author and are intended to inspire reflection, learning, and personal growth.

Author's Note

Writing this book was more than a creative project for me—it was a personal journey.

Like many people, I have experienced moments of self-doubt, fear, procrastination, and uncertainty. I know what it feels like to want growth while also feeling trapped by invisible patterns within the mind. Over time, I began to realize that many of the greatest battles we face are not external. They happen quietly within us.

This book was written to explore those inner battles.

My goal was not simply to create motivation for a few moments, but to offer ideas that encourage long-term reflection, discipline, and personal transformation. Every chapter was designed to help readers better understand themselves, challenge limiting beliefs, and develop the courage to grow beyond fear and comfort.

The lessons in this book are inspired by personal observation, research, life experiences, and the timeless principles of self-awareness and self-mastery. While no single book can transform a life overnight, I truly believe that small shifts in mindset and daily habits can create extraordinary change over time.

As you read these pages, I encourage you not to rush through the journey. Pause. Reflect. Complete the exercises. Be honest with yourself. Real transformation begins when awareness turns into action.

Most importantly, remember this:

You are not defined by your past mistakes, your fears, or your current limitations. Growth is always possible. Change is always possible. And the strength you are searching for may already exist within you.

Thank you for allowing this book to become part of your journey.

I sincerely hope it helps you climb the mountain within and discover the person you are capable of becoming.

— Asharaf Ali

TABLE OF CONTENTS

INTRODUCTION

The Battle Within

There is a silent battle happening inside every human being.

It is not a battle against the world.
It is not a battle against other people.

It is a battle within ourselves.

Every dream you have ever imagined, every goal you have ever set, and every version of the life you hope to live stands on one side of this battle.

And on the other side stands something far more powerful than any external obstacle.

Your own mind.

Many people believe their biggest problems are outside of them.

They blame circumstances.
They blame lack of resources.
They blame other people.
They blame bad luck.

But the truth is often far deeper and far more uncomfortable.

The greatest obstacle most people will ever face is the one they carry within themselves.

Self-doubt.

Fear.

Procrastination.

Overthinking.

Negative beliefs.

These invisible forces quietly shape our decisions every day.

They convince us not to try.

They whisper that we are not good enough.

They persuade us to stay comfortable instead of growing.

And without realizing it, we slowly begin to sabotage our own lives.

This is called **self-sabotage**.

Self-sabotage does not look dramatic.
It does not announce itself loudly.

It appears in small moments.

The moment you delay starting something important.

The moment you give up too quickly.

The moment you tell yourself you will try again "tomorrow."

The moment you choose comfort instead of progress.

These moments seem small, but over time they shape our entire future.

Many people spend years wondering why they are not moving forward.

They work hard.

They dream big.

They want success.

Yet something always seems to hold them back.

It feels like climbing a mountain while carrying invisible weight.

Step by step, the climb becomes exhausting.

Eventually, many people stop trying.

They accept an ordinary life, not because they wanted it, but because they believe it is all they can achieve.

But here is the truth that changes everything.

The mountain standing in your way is not there to destroy you.

It is there to reveal you.

Your fears reveal what matters most to you.

Your struggles reveal your strength.

Your challenges reveal the person you are capable of becoming.

Inside every obstacle lies an opportunity for transformation.

This book is about understanding the mountain within you.

It is about discovering why we sabotage ourselves and how we can break free from the patterns that keep us stuck.

It is about turning fear into courage.

Turning confusion into clarity.

Turning weakness into strength.

But most importantly, it is about becoming the person you were always capable of being.

Because the truth is simple.

You are not broken.

You are not incapable.

You are not meant to remain stuck where you are.

You simply have patterns that must be understood.

Habits that must be changed.

Beliefs that must be challenged.

Once you begin to understand yourself deeply, everything begins to shift.

You stop fighting yourself.

You start working with your mind instead of against it.

You begin to build discipline, clarity, and inner strength.

And slowly, the mountain that once seemed impossible to climb becomes the very path that leads you to your greatest potential.

The journey ahead will challenge you.

It will ask you to confront your fears.

It will ask you to question the stories you have been telling yourself for years.

But it will also show you something extraordinary.

That the power to transform your life has always been within you.

The mountain you must climb is not outside.

It is within.

And once you learn how to rise above it, there will be no limit to how far you can go.

Welcome to the journey of **self-mastery**.

CHAPTER 1

The Mountain Within You

Every human being carries a mountain within.

Some people spend their entire lives trying to climb mountains in the outside world — chasing success, recognition, money, or approval.

But the greatest mountain we will ever face is not outside.

It is inside us.

It is built from our fears, doubts, habits, and beliefs.

It is the quiet voice that says,
"Maybe you are not good enough."

It is the hesitation that appears just before you take a bold step forward.

It is the invisible force that pulls you back every time you begin to move toward something bigger.

This mountain is called **self-sabotage**.

Self-sabotage is not always obvious. It rarely appears in dramatic ways.

Instead, it hides in small daily choices.

You delay starting something important.

You make excuses when opportunities appear.

You doubt your abilities even when you are capable.

You abandon goals that once excited you.

These actions may seem small, but over time they build the mountain higher and higher.

The most dangerous part of self-sabotage is that we often believe it is normal.

We convince ourselves that we are simply being "realistic."

We tell ourselves things like:

"I am not ready yet."
"I will start when the time is right."
"What if I fail?"

But deep inside, we know the truth.

The real problem is not lack of opportunity.

It is lack of belief.

It is fear disguised as logic.

And until we recognize the mountain within us, we will continue to walk in circles around it.

Why the Mountain Exists

Your mind was designed for survival, not success.

Thousands of years ago, humans survived by avoiding danger and staying within safe limits.

Taking risks could mean losing food, shelter, or even life.

Because of this, the brain developed a powerful instinct: **avoid discomfort.**

Even today, this instinct remains.

Your brain still treats uncertainty as a threat.

Trying something new feels uncomfortable.

Speaking up feels risky.

Chasing a big dream feels dangerous.

So the mind tries to protect you.

It tells you to wait.

It tells you to stay where you are.

It tells you to choose comfort instead of growth.

But comfort is often the very thing that keeps people stuck.

Growth requires uncertainty.

Progress requires discomfort.

Transformation requires courage.

The mountain exists because the mind prefers safety over possibility.

But once you understand this truth, something powerful happens.

You stop believing every thought your mind produces.

You begin to question your fears.

You begin to see the difference between real danger and imagined limitation.

And slowly, the mountain begins to shrink.

The Illusion of Being Stuck

Many people believe they are stuck in life.

They believe their situation cannot change.

They believe they are limited by their background, their past, or their abilities.

But in reality, most people are not stuck.

They are simply **unaware of the patterns controlling them.**

Patterns shape everything.

The way you think.

The way you react.

The way you make decisions.

If someone repeatedly delays important work, it becomes a pattern.

If someone constantly doubts themselves, it becomes a pattern.

If someone avoids challenges, it becomes a pattern.

Over time, patterns turn into identity.

You begin to say things like:

"I'm just not confident."
"I'm not disciplined."
"I'm not the type of person who succeeds."

But these are not truths.

They are habits repeated so often that they feel permanent.

The moment you realize that your identity is built from patterns, you gain the power to change it.

Because patterns can be broken.

And new ones can be created.

The First Step Toward Self-Mastery

The first step in climbing your inner mountain is **awareness.**

Most people live their lives on autopilot.

They react instead of reflecting.

They follow habits without questioning them.

But the moment you begin observing your thoughts and actions, everything changes.

You begin to notice when fear is guiding your decisions.

You begin to notice when procrastination appears.

You begin to notice when your mind is trying to keep you small.

This awareness is powerful.

Because you cannot change something you do not see.

But once you see it clearly, you can begin to transform it.

Self-mastery does not happen overnight.

It happens through small moments of awareness repeated every day.

Each moment you choose courage instead of comfort.

Each moment you act despite fear.

Each moment you take responsibility for your choices.

These moments slowly reshape who you are.

And before long, the mountain that once seemed impossible begins to feel climbable.

Not because the mountain disappeared.

But because **you became stronger.**

Chapter 1 Activities

Activity 1: Identify Your Mountain

Take a moment to reflect honestly.

Write down the biggest obstacles in your life right now.

Ask yourself:

- What fear holds me back the most?
- What habit repeatedly stops my progress?
- What goal have I been avoiding?

Write your answers clearly.

Naming the mountain is the first step toward climbing it.

Activity 2: The Self-Sabotage Reflection

Think about a time when you stopped yourself from doing something important.

Ask yourself:

- What thoughts appeared in my mind?
- What emotions did I feel?
- What decision did I make because of those thoughts?

Understanding your patterns will help you break them.

Activity 3: The Awareness Exercise

For the next **three days**, observe your thoughts carefully.

Every time you notice:

- self-doubt
- procrastination
- fear of trying

Write it down.

Do not judge yourself.

Simply observe.

Awareness is the beginning of transformation.

Chapter Reflection

The mountain within you is not your enemy.

It is a mirror.

It shows you where fear lives.

It shows you where growth is waiting.

And once you begin climbing it, step by step, you will discover something extraordinary.

The person standing at the top of that mountain…

is the person you were always meant to become.

CHAPTER 2

Understanding Self-Sabotage

Most people believe that when they fail to reach their goals, something outside of them is responsible.

They blame time.
They blame circumstances.
They blame other people.
They blame bad luck.

But if we look honestly at our lives, we often discover a deeper truth.

Many of the obstacles we face are not created by the world around us.

They are created by the patterns within us.

This is the quiet and powerful force called **self-sabotage**.

Self-sabotage happens when your actions, habits, or decisions prevent you from achieving what you truly want.

It is the strange moment when a person dreams of success but behaves in ways that lead to failure.

It is the moment when someone wants to grow, yet continues to choose comfort.

It is when a person knows what they should do, but still does the opposite.

This contradiction confuses many people.

Why would someone block their own progress?

Why would someone sabotage their own happiness?

The answer is deeper than laziness or lack of motivation.

Self-sabotage is often a **protection mechanism created by the mind**.

Your mind tries to protect you from emotional pain.

It tries to protect you from rejection, embarrassment, failure, and uncertainty.

But sometimes the protection becomes a prison.

Instead of protecting you, it keeps you stuck.

The Hidden Fear Behind Self-Sabotage

At the core of self-sabotage is **fear**.

Not always obvious fear.

Often quiet, hidden fear.

Fear of failure.

Fear of judgment.

Fear of rejection.

Fear of not being good enough.

But there is another fear that many people do not talk about.

The **fear of success**.

Success brings change.

Success brings responsibility.

Success brings visibility.

When life changes, expectations increase.

Some people unconsciously avoid success because they fear the pressure that comes with it.

So the mind creates subtle ways to escape.

Procrastination.

Overthinking.

Perfectionism.

Distraction.

These behaviors feel harmless in the moment.

But over time, they quietly destroy progress.

The Patterns That Keep People Stuck

Self-sabotage rarely happens once.

It happens repeatedly.

That is because it forms **patterns**.

Patterns are habits of thought and behavior that repeat over time.

The more often they repeat, the stronger they become.

Here are some of the most common self-sabotage patterns.

1. Procrastination

Procrastination is one of the most common forms of self-sabotage.

People delay tasks not because they are lazy, but because they feel uncomfortable.

Starting something important creates pressure.

It creates the possibility of failure.

So the mind chooses temporary relief.

"I will do it later."

But later becomes tomorrow.

Tomorrow becomes next week.

And progress disappears.

2. Perfectionism

Perfectionism appears positive on the surface.

But often it hides fear.

People who wait for perfection rarely begin.

They spend too much time preparing.

Too much time planning.

Too much time worrying about mistakes.

But growth never happens in perfect conditions.

Growth happens through action.

3. Negative Self-Talk

The words you speak to yourself shape your identity.

Many people carry an inner voice that constantly criticizes them.

"You are not smart enough."

"You will fail."

"You cannot do this."

Over time, these thoughts become beliefs.

And beliefs shape behavior.

If you believe you will fail, you stop trying.

If you believe you are not capable, you avoid challenges.

This is how self-sabotage becomes a cycle.

The Emotional Roots of Self-Sabotage

Behind every sabotaging habit lies an emotional reason.

Often these reasons come from past experiences.

A person who faced criticism may fear judgment.

A person who experienced failure may fear trying again.

A person who was ignored may fear being seen.

The mind remembers these experiences and tries to avoid repeating the pain.

But avoiding pain also means avoiding growth.

True progress begins when we stop running from discomfort and start learning from it.

Awareness Changes Everything

The most powerful weapon against self-sabotage is **awareness**.

When you become aware of your patterns, they lose their power.

You begin to notice when fear appears.

You recognize when procrastination is trying to protect you.

You see when your mind is creating excuses.

This awareness gives you a choice.

Instead of reacting automatically, you can respond intentionally.

Instead of repeating old patterns, you can create new ones.

Self-mastery begins with this simple shift.

From unconscious behavior to conscious decision.

The moment you begin observing your mind, you begin reclaiming control over your life.

Chapter 2 Activities

Activity 1: Discover Your Self-Sabotage Pattern

Take a few minutes to reflect on your life.

Answer these questions honestly:

- What goal have I been delaying the most?
- What excuses do I usually make?
- What emotion do I feel when I think about starting?

Write your answers in detail.

This will help you identify your personal self-sabotage pattern.

Activity 2: The Fear Identification Exercise

Many forms of self-sabotage are driven by fear.

Ask yourself:

- What am I afraid might happen if I succeed?
- What am I afraid might happen if I fail?
- What judgment from others do I fear the most?

Write your answers without filtering them.

Understanding your fears weakens their control over you.

Activity 3: The Thought Awareness Practice

For the next **five days**, pay attention to your thoughts.

Whenever you notice a negative thought such as:

• "I cannot do this."
• "I will fail."
• "I am not ready."

Write it down.

Next to it, write a more balanced thought, such as:

"I may struggle, but I can learn."
"I can improve with practice."
"I can start even if I am not perfect."

This simple practice begins to reshape your thinking.

Chapter Reflection

Self-sabotage is not proof that you are weak.

It is proof that your mind has been trying to protect you.

But protection without growth becomes limitation.

When you begin to understand your fears, your patterns, and your thoughts, something powerful happens.

The behaviors that once controlled you start to lose their grip.

And the person who once stood in their own way begins to move forward with clarity and courage.

Understanding self-sabotage is not the end of the journey.

It is the beginning of freedom.

CHAPTER 3

Why Your Mind Works Against You

Have you ever promised yourself that you would change something in your life?

You decided you would wake up early.

You decided you would stop procrastinating.

You decided you would work harder on your goals.

In that moment, everything felt clear.

You felt motivated.

You felt determined.

But a few days later, something strange happened.

Your motivation faded.

Your energy disappeared.

You returned to the same habits you wanted to change.

And once again, you felt frustrated with yourself.

Many people interpret this as weakness.

They believe they lack discipline.

They believe something is wrong with them.

But the truth is far more interesting.

Your mind is not broken.

Your mind is simply doing what it was designed to do.

Your brain was not built for success.

It was built for **survival**.

Understanding this truth can change the way you see yourself forever.

The Brain's First Priority: Survival

Thousands of years ago, human beings lived in dangerous environments.

Every day was uncertain.

Food was limited.

Predators were everywhere.

Survival depended on avoiding risk.

Because of this, the human brain developed a powerful instinct.

It constantly searches for danger.

Anything unfamiliar or uncertain can trigger a warning signal.

Even today, your brain still carries this ancient survival system.

But here is the problem.

The world has changed.

We no longer live in jungles surrounded by predators.

But our brain still reacts as if we do.

Today, the "danger" is not a wild animal.

It might be:

- speaking in front of people
- starting a business
- sharing your ideas
- trying something new

Your brain interprets these situations as threats.

And when the brain senses danger, it tries to protect you.

It does this by pushing you back into comfort.

The Comfort Zone Trap

Your comfort zone is not a place.

It is a mental boundary.

Inside this boundary, everything feels familiar and predictable.

Your brain feels safe here.

The problem is that **growth never happens inside the comfort zone.**

Growth happens in uncertainty.

Growth happens when you try something unfamiliar.

Growth happens when you risk failure.

But when you step outside your comfort zone, your brain reacts with resistance.

You feel:

- fear
- anxiety
- self-doubt
- hesitation

These feelings are not signs that you should stop.

They are signs that you are entering a new level of growth.

Unfortunately, many people misunderstand this feeling.

They think discomfort means something is wrong.

So they retreat back into comfort.

And the cycle continues.

Why Habits Are So Hard to Change

Habits are powerful because they save the brain energy.

Your brain prefers automatic behavior.

When you repeat an action many times, the brain creates a shortcut.

This shortcut allows you to perform the action without thinking.

That is why brushing your teeth feels automatic.

Driving a familiar route feels easy.

The same process happens with negative habits.

Procrastination becomes automatic.

Overthinking becomes automatic.

Avoiding challenges becomes automatic.

These patterns become deeply wired into the brain.

Changing them requires effort because you are asking the brain to create a new pathway.

At first, the brain resists.

It prefers the old pattern because it requires less energy.

But here is the powerful truth.

The brain is capable of change.

This ability is called **neuroplasticity**.

Neuroplasticity means your brain can build new connections and weaken old ones.

Every time you repeat a new behavior, you strengthen a new pathway.

Every time you resist an old habit, you weaken the old pathway.

Change does not happen instantly.

But with repetition, transformation becomes inevitable.

Reprogramming Your Mind

If your mind has been trained by years of habits and beliefs, then change requires **intentional retraining**.

This does not happen through motivation alone.

It happens through consistent small actions.

Small actions repeated daily reshape the brain.

Every time you choose progress over comfort, you are rewiring your mind.

Every time you act despite fear, you are strengthening courage.

The key is not perfection.

The key is **consistency**.

Chapter 3 Activities

Activity 1: The Comfort Zone Map

Take a piece of paper and draw three circles.

Label them:

Circle 1: Comfort Zone
Circle 2: Growth Zone
Circle 3: Fear Zone

Now answer these questions.

Comfort Zone:
• What activities feel easy and familiar in my life?

Growth Zone:
• What actions could improve my life but feel slightly uncomfortable?

Fear Zone:
• What goals feel intimidating but exciting?

This exercise helps you see where your growth truly lies.

Activity 2: The Habit Awareness Exercise

For the next **seven days**, observe your habits carefully.

Each evening write down:

• One habit that helped your progress
• One habit that slowed your progress

After seven days, look at the patterns.

This awareness is the first step to changing habits.

Activity 3: The Small Action Rule

Choose **one small action** that moves you toward your goal.

Make it extremely simple.

For example:

• write for 10 minutes
• read 5 pages

- exercise for 10 minutes
- work on your project for 15 minutes

Do this every day for **30 days**.

Small consistent actions create powerful long-term change.

Activity 4: The Fear Reframing Exercise

Think about a fear that has been holding you back.

Write answers to these questions:

- What is the worst thing that could happen?
- How likely is it to actually happen?
- If it happens, how would I handle it?

Most fears lose power when we examine them logically.

Chapter Reflection

Your mind is not your enemy.

It is simply following the patterns it has learned.

The brain prefers safety.

It prefers comfort.

It prefers familiar routines.

But you are not controlled by these patterns.

You are capable of reshaping them.

Every decision you make sends a message to your brain.

Every courageous action builds a stronger version of you.

At first, the mountain of change may feel steep.

But step by step, action by action, thought by thought, you begin to transform.

And eventually, the mind that once resisted growth becomes the mind that supports it.

CHAPTER 4

The Hidden Comfort of Staying the Same

At first glance, it seems strange.

Why would someone remain in a life that makes them unhappy?

Why would someone stay in habits that keep them stuck?

Why would someone continue repeating patterns that clearly do not help them grow?

Most people believe that if someone truly wants change, they will simply decide to change.

But human behavior is rarely that simple.

The truth is that people often stay stuck not because they enjoy suffering, but because **familiar pain feels safer than unfamiliar change.**

The mind prefers what it already knows.

Even when what it knows is not good for us.

This is the hidden comfort of staying the same.

The Familiar Pain

Imagine someone who has always doubted themselves.

For years, they have believed they are not capable of achieving great things.

This belief has shaped their choices.

They avoid challenges.

They hesitate to share their ideas.

They keep their dreams small.

This life may not be fulfilling.

But it feels familiar.

And familiarity creates a strange sense of comfort.

Now imagine this person suddenly decides to change.

They begin speaking confidently.

They start pursuing big goals.

They step into opportunities they once avoided.

At first, this should feel exciting.

But surprisingly, it often feels uncomfortable.

Why?

Because the mind is entering unfamiliar territory.

Even positive change can trigger fear.

This is why many people return to their old habits.

Not because they want to fail.

But because the unknown feels more frightening than the familiar.

The Identity Trap

One of the strongest forces that keeps people stuck is **identity**.

Identity is the story we tell ourselves about who we are.

Over time, these stories become deeply rooted.

A person might believe:

"I am not disciplined."

"I am not confident."

"I am not the type of person who succeeds."

These statements may feel like facts.

But they are actually **beliefs formed by repeated experiences.**

The problem begins when people attach themselves to these identities.

They begin to live according to them.

If someone believes they are not disciplined, they avoid situations that require discipline.

If someone believes they are not confident, they avoid situations that require confidence.

The belief becomes a self-fulfilling prophecy.

The more they repeat the behavior, the stronger the identity becomes.

But here is an important truth.

Your identity is not permanent.

It is simply a collection of habits, beliefs, and experiences.

And anything built through repetition can be rebuilt through new repetition.

The Illusion of Comfort

Comfort often appears peaceful on the surface.

It feels easy.

It feels safe.

It feels predictable.

But comfort can quietly turn into a trap.

When people stay in comfort too long, growth stops.

Dreams become smaller.

Confidence slowly fades.

Opportunities pass by unnoticed.

The person may not feel extreme pain, but they feel something else.

A quiet dissatisfaction.

A sense that life could be more.

A feeling that they are capable of something greater.

This feeling is not random.

It is the voice of potential.

It is the part of you that knows you were not meant to stay small.

Ignoring this voice may bring temporary comfort.

But over time, it leads to regret.

Because the greatest regret in life is rarely failure.

The greatest regret is **never trying.**

Breaking the Comfort Illusion

Breaking free from the comfort illusion requires courage.

It requires accepting that growth will feel uncomfortable.

It requires stepping into uncertainty.

But discomfort is not the enemy.

Discomfort is often the doorway to transformation.

Every skill you admire in others was built through discomfort.

Every successful person you respect has faced moments of fear.

Growth is rarely smooth.

It involves mistakes.

It involves learning.

It involves persistence.

But on the other side of that discomfort lies something powerful.

Freedom.

Freedom from the patterns that once controlled you.

Freedom from the beliefs that once limited you.

Freedom to create a life that truly reflects your potential.

Chapter 4 Activities

Activity 1: The Comfort Zone Reflection

Take a few minutes and answer these questions honestly.

- What areas of my life feel comfortable but unfulfilling?
- What dreams have I avoided because they feel uncertain?
- What opportunities have I ignored due to fear?

Write your answers clearly.

This exercise will help you recognize where comfort may be limiting your growth.

Activity 2: The Identity Rewrite Exercise

Write down three beliefs you currently hold about yourself.

For example:

"I am not disciplined."
"I am not confident."
"I am not good at communication."

Now rewrite each belief into a new empowering identity.

Example:

"I am becoming more disciplined every day."
"I am learning to speak with confidence."
"I am improving my communication skills."

Repeat these new identities daily.

Your mind begins to believe what it hears repeatedly.

Activity 3: The Discomfort Challenge

Choose **one small action** that makes you slightly uncomfortable but helps your growth.

Examples:

- speaking up in a meeting
- sharing your ideas online
- starting a project you have been delaying
- approaching a new opportunity

Commit to doing this action within the next **48 hours.**

Growth begins the moment you act despite discomfort.

Activity 4: The Future Vision Exercise

Close your eyes and imagine your life **five years from now** if you continue staying the same.

How would you feel?

What opportunities might you miss?

Now imagine your life five years from now if you choose growth.

What could become possible?

Write both visions in detail.

This exercise helps you see the real cost of staying the same.

Chapter Reflection

The comfort zone is seductive.

It whispers promises of safety.

It offers the illusion of peace.

But beneath that comfort often lies stagnation.

Growth begins when you challenge the familiar.

When you question the identities you have carried for years.

When you step into uncertainty with courage.

You do not need to change everything overnight.

You only need to take one step beyond comfort.

Then another.

And another.

With each step, the life that once seemed distant begins to move closer.

Because the moment you stop hiding inside comfort…

you begin becoming the person you were meant to be.

CHAPTER 5

Fear — The Silent Controller

Fear rarely announces itself loudly.

It does not always appear as panic or trembling.

Most of the time, fear moves quietly through our thoughts and decisions, shaping our lives without us even realizing it.

It whispers in subtle ways.

"Maybe this is not the right time."
"What if people judge you?"
"You might fail."

These whispers seem harmless.

But over time, they become powerful enough to guide our choices.

Fear becomes the silent controller of our lives.

Many people believe they are making logical decisions when, in reality, they are simply obeying their fears.

They choose safe paths instead of meaningful ones.

They avoid challenges that could transform them.

They silence their dreams before those dreams even have a chance to grow.

Fear is not always visible.

But its influence can be found in almost every important decision we make.

Understanding fear is the first step toward reclaiming control.

How Fear Secretly Controls Decisions

Fear rarely says, *"I am controlling you."*

Instead, it disguises itself as reason.

You may tell yourself:

"I need more preparation."

"I will start next month."

"I should wait until the situation is perfect."

These thoughts sound practical.

But often they are simply fear wearing the mask of logic.

Fear convinces you that waiting is wise.

Fear convinces you that trying is risky.

Fear convinces you that staying small is safe.

And slowly, without noticing, your life becomes shaped by avoidance.

The opportunities you never take.

The ideas you never share.

The dreams you never pursue.

Each of these moments represents a quiet victory for fear.

But fear only gains power when it remains unchallenged.

The moment you recognize it, you weaken its control.

The Fear of Failure

One of the most common fears people experience is the fear of failure.

Failure can feel painful.

It can bring embarrassment.

It can invite criticism from others.

Because of this, many people prefer not to try at all.

They believe avoiding failure protects them.

But this belief creates a dangerous trap.

When people avoid failure, they also avoid growth.

Every skill, every achievement, and every success requires mistakes along the way.

Failure is not the opposite of success.

It is part of the process that leads to success.

Think of a child learning to walk.

The child falls many times.

Yet each fall teaches balance.

Each attempt builds strength.

Eventually, walking becomes natural.

Adults forget this process.

They expect success without mistakes.

And when failure appears, they interpret it as proof that they should stop.

But the truth is simple.

Failure is feedback.

It shows you what needs improvement.

It reveals where growth is required.

And when viewed with the right mindset, failure becomes one of the most powerful teachers in life.

The Fear of Success

While fear of failure is widely recognized, there is another fear that many people overlook.

The fear of success.

At first, this idea seems strange.

Why would someone fear success?

But success brings change.

It brings attention.

It brings expectations.

When someone succeeds, others begin to watch them.

People expect more.

Responsibility increases.

For some individuals, this attention feels overwhelming.

They fear being judged.

They fear losing relationships.

They fear that success might isolate them.

Because of these hidden fears, the mind sometimes chooses sabotage.

A person may delay their progress.

They may abandon opportunities.

They may unconsciously hold themselves back.

Not because they do not want success.

But because they fear what success might bring.

Recognizing this hidden fear allows you to confront it directly.

Success does not need to isolate you.

Success simply expands your potential.

Turning Fear Into Courage

Fear will always exist.

It is a natural part of being human.

But courage is not the absence of fear.

Courage is the decision to act despite it.

Every courageous person you admire has faced fear.

The difference is that they refused to let fear make their decisions.

They understood something powerful.

Fear often appears strongest right before a breakthrough.

It stands at the edge of growth.

It guards the doorway to new possibilities.

When you walk through that doorway, fear loses its power.

And confidence begins to grow.

Confidence is not something you are born with.

It is something you build through action.

Each time you face fear, you strengthen your belief in yourself.

Each time you act despite doubt, you expand your comfort zone.

Over time, courage becomes part of your identity.

Chapter 5 Activities

Activity 1: Identify Your Biggest Fear

Take a moment to reflect deeply.

Ask yourself:

- What fear has been holding me back the most?
- What goal have I avoided because of this fear?
- How long has this fear influenced my decisions?

Write your answers honestly.

Clarity is the first step toward courage.

Activity 2: The Fear Breakdown Exercise

Choose one fear and examine it carefully.

Write down:

- What exactly am I afraid of?
- What is the worst realistic outcome?
- If that outcome happens, how would I recover?

Most fears become smaller when we analyze them logically.

Activity 3: The Courage Action Challenge

Select one action that fear has been preventing you from taking.

Make it small but meaningful.

Examples:

- sharing an idea
- starting a project
- contacting someone for an opportunity
- speaking up in a discussion

Commit to taking this action within the next **24 hours**.

Action weakens fear faster than thinking.

Activity 4: The Courage Journal

For the next **seven days**, record one moment each day when you act despite fear.

It does not have to be a big action.

Even small acts of courage count.

At the end of the week, review your journal.

You will begin to see a new version of yourself emerging.

Chapter Reflection

Fear is powerful, but it is not invincible.

It grows stronger when ignored.

It grows weaker when confronted.

Every great transformation begins with a moment of courage.

A moment when someone decides that their dreams are more important than their fears.

You do not need to eliminate fear to move forward.

You only need the courage to take the next step.

And once you take that step, you will discover something remarkable.

The path you once feared…

was the path that was always meant to lead you forward.

CHAPTER 6

Breaking the Cycle of Negative Patterns

Many people promise themselves that they will change.

They decide they will stop procrastinating.

They promise they will become more disciplined.

They tell themselves that tomorrow will be different.

But tomorrow arrives…

and the same habits return.

The same thoughts appear.

The same patterns repeat.

This cycle can feel frustrating.

It can make people question their willpower.

It can make them feel as if they are trapped in a loop they cannot escape.

But the truth is important to understand.

People do not repeat destructive patterns because they want to fail.

They repeat them because **patterns become automatic over time**.

Once a pattern is deeply wired into the brain, it begins to run like a program.

You no longer need to think about it.

Your mind simply follows the familiar path.

Understanding how these patterns work is the first step toward breaking them.

Why People Repeat Destructive Habits

Every habit follows a simple psychological loop.

It begins with a **trigger**.

The trigger creates an emotional response.

That emotion leads to a **behavior**.

And that behavior creates a short-term reward.

Over time, this cycle becomes automatic.

For example:

A person feels stressed.
Stress becomes the trigger.

To escape the stress, they procrastinate or distract themselves.

The distraction provides temporary relief.

The brain remembers this relief.

So the next time stress appears, the brain repeats the same behavior.

This is how destructive patterns are created.

The brain learns what provides quick comfort.

Even if that comfort creates long-term problems.

Because the brain prioritizes immediate relief over future success.

Breaking these cycles requires interrupting the pattern.

The Mental Loop

Negative patterns are often strengthened by mental loops.

A mental loop is a repeated chain of thoughts that reinforces the same behavior.

For example:

A person wants to start a project.

But a thought appears:

"What if I fail?"

That thought creates anxiety.

The anxiety leads to avoidance.

Avoidance provides temporary relief.

The brain then reinforces the belief that avoiding the task was the right decision.

Next time, the same loop appears even faster.

Thought → Emotion → Behavior → Relief → Reinforcement.

This loop becomes stronger every time it repeats.

But there is good news.

Mental loops can be broken.

And when they are broken consistently, the brain begins to form new patterns.

The Power of Interrupting Patterns

The most powerful way to break a negative pattern is to **interrupt it**.

When the trigger appears, instead of following the usual behavior, you consciously choose a different action.

At first, this feels difficult.

Your brain will try to push you back toward the familiar response.

But every time you interrupt the pattern, you weaken the old pathway.

And you strengthen a new one.

Think of it like walking through a forest.

If you walk the same path every day, the trail becomes clear and easy.

But if you stop using that path and begin walking a new one, the old trail slowly disappears.

Your brain works in a similar way.

Old patterns fade when they are no longer used.

New patterns grow stronger with repetition.

Building Better Patterns

Breaking negative habits is only half of the process.

The other half is creating **positive patterns**.

You cannot simply remove a habit.

You must replace it.

If someone stops procrastinating but does not build a productive routine, the mind will return to its old behaviors.

Transformation happens when new habits take the place of old ones.

This process requires patience.

But small consistent actions create powerful results over time.

The key is not intensity.

The key is repetition.

A small positive action repeated daily can reshape your entire life.

Chapter 6 Activities

Activity 1: Identify Your Habit Loop

Choose one negative habit you want to change.

Answer these questions:

- What usually triggers this habit?
- What emotion do I feel before the habit begins?
- What behavior follows the emotion?
- What temporary reward does the behavior give me?

Write down your answers.

Understanding the loop makes it easier to interrupt.

Activity 2: The Pattern Interruption Plan

Once you identify the trigger, plan a new response.

Example:

Trigger: Stress from work
Old Behavior: Procrastination or distraction
New Behavior: Work for 10 minutes on the task

Write your own pattern interruption plan.

Commit to practicing it every time the trigger appears.

Activity 3: The Two-Minute Rule

Many habits fail because the starting point feels too difficult.

The solution is to make the beginning extremely small.

Choose a habit and reduce it to **two minutes**.

Examples:

- Write for two minutes
- Read for two minutes
- Exercise for two minutes

Starting is the hardest part.

Once you begin, continuing becomes easier.

Activity 4: The Weekly Pattern Review

At the end of each week, ask yourself:

- Which habits improved my life this week?
- Which habits slowed my progress?
- What pattern do I want to improve next week?

Write your answers in a journal.

This reflection builds awareness and accountability.

Chapter Reflection

Negative patterns are not permanent.

They are simply habits repeated long enough to feel automatic.

Every pattern in your life was created through repetition.

And anything created through repetition can be changed the same way.

The process requires patience.

It requires awareness.

And most importantly, it requires consistency.

Each time you interrupt a negative pattern, you take a step toward freedom.

Each time you replace it with a positive action, you strengthen the person you want to become.

At first, the change may feel small.

But small actions repeated over time create extraordinary transformation.

Because the life you build tomorrow…

begins with the patterns you change today.

CHAPTER 7

Rebuilding Your Mindset

Your life is shaped by something you rarely see.

It is not your circumstances.

It is not your resources.

It is not even your talents.

It is your **mindset**.

Mindset is the collection of beliefs you carry about yourself, your abilities, and the world around you.

These beliefs quietly influence every decision you make.

They determine whether you try or hesitate.

Whether you persist or give up.

Whether you believe growth is possible or believe you are limited.

Many people focus on changing their habits or goals, but they overlook the deeper foundation beneath those actions.

That foundation is the way they think.

If the mindset remains the same, the results will often remain the same.

True transformation begins when you rebuild the way you see yourself and your potential.

The Power of Beliefs

Every person carries beliefs about what they can and cannot do.

Some beliefs empower us.

Others quietly limit us.

These limiting beliefs often form early in life.

Perhaps someone once told you that you were not good enough.

Perhaps you experienced failure and concluded that success was not meant for you.

Perhaps you compared yourself to others and believed you could never match their abilities.

Over time, these experiences become internal beliefs.

And once a belief settles into the mind, it begins to shape behavior.

If you believe you are capable, you attempt difficult things.

If you believe you are incapable, you avoid them.

This is why beliefs are so powerful.

They act as invisible instructions that guide your actions.

But here is the most important truth.

Beliefs are not permanent facts.

They are interpretations.

And interpretations can be changed.

Transforming Limiting Beliefs

A limiting belief is a thought that convinces you that something is impossible or beyond your ability.

Examples include:

"I am not smart enough."

"I will never succeed."

"I am not disciplined."

"I am not talented."

These thoughts feel real because they have been repeated many times.

But repetition does not make them true.

To transform a limiting belief, you must first question it.

Ask yourself:

Is this belief based on evidence, or is it based on past experiences that no longer define me?

Many successful people once carried limiting beliefs.

What changed their lives was not luck or talent.

It was the decision to challenge the story they had been telling themselves.

Once a belief is challenged, it begins to weaken.

And in its place, a new belief can grow.

The Growth Mindset

Psychologists often describe two types of mindsets.

A **fixed mindset** and a **growth mindset**.

A fixed mindset believes abilities are permanent.

People with this mindset believe they are either talented or not.

They avoid challenges because failure feels like proof of weakness.

A growth mindset believes abilities can develop through effort and learning.

People with this mindset see challenges as opportunities.

They understand that mistakes are part of progress.

They do not fear failure.

They learn from it.

Developing a growth mindset transforms the way you approach life.

Instead of asking:

"What if I fail?"

You begin asking:

"What can I learn?"

Instead of believing:

"I cannot do this."

You begin believing:

"I cannot do this yet."

That single word — *yet* — opens the door to possibility.

Training Your Mind for Growth

Your mindset is like a garden.

If you do not care for it, weeds will grow naturally.

Doubt, fear, and negative beliefs can take over.

But with consistent effort, you can plant new thoughts that support growth.

Each time you challenge a limiting belief, you plant a new seed.

Each time you choose courage over doubt, you strengthen that seed.

Over time, these seeds grow into a powerful mindset that supports your goals.

The process requires patience.

But the results can transform your life.

Chapter 7 Activities

Activity 1: Identify Your Limiting Beliefs

Take time to write down three beliefs that may be limiting your growth.

Examples might include:

- "I am not confident."
- "I am not disciplined."
- "I am not good at learning new things."

Write them honestly.

Recognizing these beliefs is the first step toward changing them.

Activity 2: Challenge the Belief

Choose one limiting belief and ask yourself:

- Where did this belief come from?
- Is there real evidence that it is permanently true?
- Can I find examples that prove the opposite?

Often you will discover that your belief is not as solid as it seemed.

Activity 3: Create a New Empowering Belief

Now replace the limiting belief with a growth-oriented statement.

For example:

Limiting belief: "I am not disciplined."
New belief: "I am building discipline through small daily actions."

Repeat your new belief every day.

Your mind begins to adapt to the messages you repeat.

Activity 4: The Learning Reflection

At the end of each day, ask yourself three questions:

- What did I learn today?
- What mistake helped me grow today?
- What small improvement did I make today?

This practice strengthens a growth mindset over time.

Chapter Reflection

Your mindset is not fixed.

It is not a permanent structure.

It is a living system that evolves through your thoughts and experiences.

The beliefs you carry today were built over time.

And with intention, they can be rebuilt.

Every time you question a limiting belief, you open space for possibility.

Every time you approach challenges with curiosity instead of fear, you strengthen your growth mindset.

Transformation does not happen in a single moment.

It happens through repeated shifts in how you think, act, and respond to the world.

And once your mindset begins to change, something extraordinary happens.

The obstacles that once felt impossible begin to look like opportunities.

The person you once doubted begins to reveal their true potential.

Because when you rebuild your mindset…

you rebuild your future.

CHAPTER 8

Discipline — The Bridge to Self-Mastery

Many people wait for motivation before they begin.

They wait for the perfect mood.

They wait for the perfect moment.

They wait for the day when they feel inspired enough to take action.

But the truth is simple.

Motivation is unreliable.

Some days you feel excited and energetic.

Other days you feel tired, distracted, and doubtful.

If your progress depends on motivation, your progress will always be inconsistent.

This is where discipline becomes powerful.

Discipline does not ask how you feel.

Discipline asks what must be done.

It is the quiet decision to take action even when you do not feel like it.

It is the ability to keep moving forward when enthusiasm disappears.

And in the long run, discipline is far more powerful than motivation.

Because motivation starts the journey.

But discipline finishes it.

Why Motivation Fades

Motivation often appears at the beginning of a new goal.

You feel excited.

You imagine a better future.

You promise yourself that this time will be different.

But as days pass, the excitement fades.

The work becomes repetitive.

The progress feels slow.

And the mind begins searching for easier alternatives.

This is normal.

Motivation is emotional energy.

And emotions change constantly.

If you depend on emotions to guide your actions, your actions will change as quickly as your emotions do.

Discipline solves this problem.

Discipline replaces emotion with commitment.

It creates structure in your life.

Instead of asking, *"Do I feel like doing this today?"*

You ask, *"Is this part of the person I want to become?"*

This simple shift changes everything.

The Power of Daily Habits

Discipline is not about forcing yourself to work endlessly.

It is about creating **consistent daily habits**.

Small habits repeated every day create powerful long-term results.

Think about learning a language.

Practicing for ten minutes a day may not feel dramatic.

But after a year, those small sessions create deep knowledge.

The same principle applies to every area of life.

Fitness.

Writing.

Learning.

Business.

Confidence.

Great achievements rarely come from a single powerful effort.

They come from **small disciplined actions repeated over time**.

Habits remove the need for constant decision-making.

Once a habit is built, action becomes automatic.

And when action becomes automatic, progress becomes inevitable.

The Discipline Identity

One of the most powerful ways to build discipline is to change how you see yourself.

Instead of focusing only on goals, focus on identity.

Ask yourself:

"What kind of person do I want to become?"

Perhaps you want to become:

- a disciplined person
- a focused learner
- a reliable creator
- a healthy individual

Once you define this identity, your daily actions begin to align with it.

Each small action becomes a vote for the person you want to become.

Writing for fifteen minutes becomes a vote for being a writer.

Exercising becomes a vote for being healthy.

Studying becomes a vote for being knowledgeable.

Over time, these votes shape your identity.

And once discipline becomes part of who you are, maintaining it becomes easier.

Consistency Over Intensity

Many people fail because they try to change everything at once.

They start with extreme plans.

They work intensely for a few days.

But soon exhaustion appears.

The routine becomes overwhelming.

And they give up.

Discipline is not about extreme effort.

It is about **consistent effort**.

Small actions done every day are far more powerful than intense actions done occasionally.

Ten minutes daily is better than three hours once a week.

Consistency builds momentum.

Momentum builds confidence.

And confidence strengthens discipline.

Chapter 8 Activities

Activity 1: Define Your Discipline Identity

Write the answer to this question:

"What kind of person do I want to become?"

Examples:

- I want to become a disciplined learner.
- I want to become a focused creator.
- I want to become a healthier and stronger person.

Now ask yourself:

"What daily actions would this person take?"

Write at least three actions you can start today.

Activity 2: The Daily Habit Builder

Choose one habit that will improve your life.

Keep it small and realistic.

Examples:

- read 10 pages
- write for 10 minutes
- exercise for 15 minutes
- practice a skill daily

Commit to doing this habit for **30 days**.

Consistency matters more than intensity.

Activity 3: The No-Excuse Rule

For the next **seven days**, commit to completing one important task every day regardless of how you feel.

Do not wait for motivation.

Complete the task simply because it is part of your discipline.

At the end of the week, reflect on how this changes your mindset.

Activity 4: The Evening Discipline Reflection

At the end of each day, ask yourself three questions:

- What disciplined action did I take today?
- Where did I lose focus today?
- What will I improve tomorrow?

Write your answers in a journal.

Daily reflection strengthens discipline and awareness.

Chapter Reflection

Discipline is not something reserved for extraordinary people.

It is something built through ordinary actions repeated with consistency.

Each small action shapes the person you are becoming.

Each disciplined choice moves you closer to self-mastery.

Motivation may inspire you to begin.

But discipline will carry you forward when inspiration disappears.

And when discipline becomes part of your identity, something remarkable happens.

Progress no longer feels forced.

It becomes natural.

Because the bridge between who you are today and who you want to become…

is built with the daily steps of discipline.

CHAPTER 9

Becoming the Person You Were Meant to Be

For most of your life, you have been shaped by circumstances.

Your family.

Your environment.

Your experiences.

Your successes and failures.

All of these influences slowly built the person you are today.

Your habits formed.

Your beliefs developed.

Your identity took shape.

But something important often gets forgotten.

The person you are today is not the only version of you that can exist.

Inside every human being lives potential that has not yet been fully expressed.

A stronger version.

A wiser version.

A more confident version.

The person you are capable of becoming is often far greater than the person you currently see in the mirror.

Becoming that person does not happen by accident.

It happens through awareness, intention, and consistent growth.

And the journey toward that person begins with one powerful decision.

The decision to stop living by default…

and start living by design.

Letting Go of the Old Version of You

Transformation often begins with letting go.

Many people hold tightly to an old identity that no longer serves them.

Perhaps you once believed you were not confident.

Perhaps you believed you were not disciplined.

Perhaps you believed success was meant for others but not for you.

These beliefs may have felt true at the time.

But they do not have to define your future.

Imagine carrying a heavy backpack filled with old labels.

"I am not good enough."

"I always fail."

"I cannot change."

As long as you carry this backpack, your progress becomes difficult.

Growth requires releasing those labels.

Not by ignoring the past, but by recognizing that the past does not determine who you must become.

You are not limited to the version of yourself that existed yesterday.

You have the ability to redefine yourself today.

The Power of Personal Vision

Every meaningful transformation begins with a vision.

A clear picture of the person you want to become.

Without vision, life often moves in random directions.

But when you define your vision, your actions gain purpose.

Ask yourself:

What kind of person do I truly want to become?

Not what others expect.

Not what society suggests.

But what aligns with your deepest values.

Perhaps you want to become someone who:

- lives with discipline
- pursues meaningful goals
- helps and inspires others
- continues learning and growing

Your vision becomes a compass.

It guides your decisions.

It reminds you why your efforts matter.

And when challenges appear, your vision gives you the strength to continue.

Growth Is a Lifelong Journey

Becoming your best self is not a single moment of success.

It is an ongoing process.

There will be times when progress feels slow.

There will be moments when doubt returns.

There will be days when you feel like giving up.

But growth is not measured by perfection.

It is measured by persistence.

Every small improvement matters.

Every lesson learned matters.

Every step forward matters.

Over time, these small improvements create extraordinary change.

The person you become after years of consistent growth may be unrecognizable compared to the person you once were.

And that transformation begins with daily choices.

Living With Intention

When you choose growth, you begin living intentionally.

You no longer allow fear or habit to control your direction.

Instead, you take responsibility for your actions.

You begin asking powerful questions:

"What decision will move me closer to my best self?"

"What habit will help me grow?"

"What action reflects the person I want to become?"

Living intentionally does not mean life becomes easy.

But it does mean your life becomes meaningful.

And meaning gives strength even during difficult moments.

Chapter 9 Activities

Activity 1: The Future Self Vision

Imagine yourself **five years from now** living your ideal life.

Ask yourself:

• What kind of person have I become?
• What habits define my daily life?
• What accomplishments make me proud?

Write this vision in detail.

The clearer your vision becomes, the easier it is to move toward it.

Activity 2: The Identity Alignment Exercise

Write down three qualities of the person you want to become.

For example:

• disciplined
• confident
• focused

Now ask yourself:

"What daily actions would this person take?"

Write one action you can start practicing today for each quality.

Activity 3: The Letting Go Exercise

Write down three limiting labels you have carried about yourself.

Examples:

- "I am not confident."
- "I always procrastinate."
- "I am not capable."

Now rewrite each statement as a growth identity.

Example:

"I am learning to act with confidence."

Repeat these new statements regularly.

Activity 4: The Daily Progress Journal

At the end of each day, answer these questions:

- What action today helped me become my best self?
- What lesson did I learn today?
- What will I improve tomorrow?

Small reflections create powerful awareness.

Chapter Reflection

Becoming the person you were meant to be is not about perfection.

It is about progress.

It is about choosing growth even when comfort is easier.

It is about believing that the person you are today is only the beginning of what you can become.

Every step you take toward self-awareness, discipline, courage, and growth shapes a new identity.

Slowly, the old version of you fades.

And a stronger version emerges.

Not because life suddenly became easier.

But because you chose to rise above the limits that once held you back.

And when you continue this journey with patience and purpose…

you begin to realize something extraordinary.

The person you once dreamed of becoming…

is slowly becoming the person you truly are.

CHAPTER 10

Turning Your Mountain Into Your Strength

Every person faces mountains in life.

Some mountains appear as fear.

Some appear as failure.

Some appear as doubt, struggle, or uncertainty.

At first, these mountains seem like obstacles placed in our path.

They slow us down.

They test our patience.

They make the journey feel difficult.

Many people spend their lives wishing these mountains did not exist.

They hope life will become easier.

They hope challenges will disappear.

But the truth is something far more powerful.

The mountains in your life are not meant to block you.

They are meant to **shape you**.

Every challenge you face has the potential to build strength within you.

Every obstacle contains a lesson.

Every struggle carries the possibility of transformation.

The question is not whether mountains will appear in your life.

The real question is how you choose to respond when they do.

The Power of Perspective

Two people can face the same difficulty and experience completely different outcomes.

One person may see the challenge as proof that life is unfair.

They feel defeated.

They give up.

The other person may see the challenge as an opportunity.

They ask:

"What can this teach me?"

"How can I grow stronger from this experience?"

The difference between these two people is not talent or intelligence.

The difference is perspective.

Perspective changes everything.

When you begin to view challenges as opportunities for growth, the meaning of difficulty changes.

Failure becomes feedback.

Fear becomes a signal of growth.

Obstacles become stepping stones.

The mountain that once seemed impossible begins to reveal a path forward.

Strength Is Built Through Struggle

Think about the strongest people you know.

The people who inspire others.

The people who remain calm during difficult moments.

The people who continue moving forward even when circumstances are hard.

These individuals were not born with strength.

Their strength was built.

Built through challenges.

Built through failures.

Built through moments when quitting would have been easier.

Struggle shapes character.

Each time you face difficulty and continue anyway, something inside you grows stronger.

Resilience.

Patience.

Wisdom.

Confidence.

Over time, the very struggles you once feared become the experiences that define your strength.

Turning Pain Into Purpose

Many of the most inspiring people in the world have transformed their struggles into something meaningful.

They turned pain into motivation.

They turned failure into lessons.

They turned obstacles into opportunities to help others.

Your challenges can do the same.

The difficulties you face today may one day become the wisdom you share with someone else.

The lessons you learn today may guide someone who is walking the same path tomorrow.

Your mountain can become more than a challenge.

It can become a source of strength, understanding, and purpose.

The Journey Never Truly Ends

Personal growth is not a destination.

It is a lifelong journey.

Even when you overcome one mountain, another may appear.

But something important changes along the way.

You become stronger.

You become wiser.

You begin to trust yourself.

The mountains that once felt overwhelming become challenges you know you can face.

Because you have already climbed before.

Each climb prepares you for the next.

And with every step, you become more capable of creating the life you desire.

Chapter 10 Activities

Activity 1: Reflect on Your Mountain

Take a moment to reflect on the biggest challenge you have faced in your life.

Ask yourself:

- What did this experience teach me?
- How did it change the way I see myself?
- What strength did I develop because of it?

Write your answers honestly.

Often the most difficult moments teach the most valuable lessons.

Activity 2: Reframing Your Current Challenge

Think about a challenge you are currently facing.

Instead of asking:

"Why is this happening to me?"

Ask:

"What can this experience teach me?"
"How can this challenge make me stronger?"

Write down at least three lessons this situation might offer.

Activity 3: The Strength List

Make a list of personal strengths you have developed over the years.

Examples might include:

- resilience
- patience
- determination
- courage

Recognizing your strengths helps you approach future challenges with confidence.

Activity 4: The Next Mountain Plan

Write down one goal that feels challenging but meaningful.

Break it into small steps.

Step 1: What action can I take this week?
Step 2: What action can I take this month?
Step 3: What progress do I hope to see within one year?

Every mountain becomes manageable when broken into smaller steps.

Final Reflection

The mountain you once feared may not disappear.

But your relationship with it can change.

What once seemed impossible can become a challenge you are ready to face.

What once felt like a burden can become a source of strength.

You now understand something many people never realize.

Your fears do not define you.

Your past does not limit you.

Your struggles do not weaken you.

They shape you.

They prepare you.

They reveal the strength that has always existed within you.

Every step you take toward growth proves something powerful.

You are capable of change.

You are capable of resilience.

You are capable of becoming more than you once believed.

The mountain was never meant to stop you.

It was meant to show you how strong you truly are.

And now that you know this truth…

the path forward is yours to climb.

Conclusion

The Journey Continues

By now, you have traveled through an important journey.

A journey not across cities or countries, but through the landscape of your own mind.

You have explored the mountains within you.

You have examined fear, self-doubt, and the patterns that quietly shape your life.

You have learned how the mind works, why habits form, and how discipline builds strength.

You have discovered that many of the obstacles you once believed were permanent were simply patterns waiting to be changed.

This journey may have begun with a simple idea.

The idea that the greatest mountain in your life might not exist in the outside world.

It exists within you.

But as you continued reading, another truth began to emerge.

The mountain within you is not only an obstacle.

It is also an opportunity.

An opportunity to grow.

An opportunity to understand yourself more deeply.

An opportunity to become stronger than you were yesterday.

Throughout this book, you have seen how fear can influence decisions, how comfort can hold people back, and how habits can quietly control daily actions.

But you have also learned something far more powerful.

You have learned that these forces are not permanent.

They can be understood.

They can be challenged.

And they can be transformed.

Change does not happen overnight.

It happens through awareness.

It happens through small decisions repeated every day.

It happens when you choose growth instead of comfort.

When you choose courage instead of fear.

When you choose discipline instead of delay.

Each small choice shapes the person you are becoming.

And over time, those choices create extraordinary transformation.

There will still be moments when doubt appears.

There will still be days when progress feels slow.

There will still be challenges that test your patience and strength.

But now you understand something important.

Challenges are not the end of the journey.

They are part of the path.

Each obstacle carries a lesson.

Each struggle builds resilience.

Each step forward reveals new possibilities.

The goal of this book was never to promise an easy life.

Life will always contain uncertainty.

Life will always contain challenges.

But what can change is the way you face those challenges.

Instead of seeing mountains as barriers, you can begin to see them as opportunities to climb higher.

Instead of allowing fear to control your direction, you can use courage to guide your actions.

Instead of repeating old patterns, you can create new ones.

This is the essence of self-mastery.

Self-mastery does not mean controlling everything in life.

It means learning to guide your thoughts, your habits, and your choices with intention.

It means becoming the author of your own story.

Every day offers a new page.

Every decision writes a new sentence.

And every action shapes the future you are creating.

The person you will become five years from now will be shaped by the choices you make starting today.

So ask yourself one simple question:

What kind of story do you want to write?

Do you want a story of hesitation and regret?

Or a story of courage, growth, and possibility?

The answer begins with the next step you take.

The mountain is still there.

But now you see it differently.

It is no longer something standing in your way.

It is something inviting you to rise.

And as you continue climbing, you may discover something extraordinary.

The strength you were searching for…

was within you all along.

Your journey has only just begun.

BIBLIOGRAPHY

The ideas and principles explored in this book are inspired by established works in personal development, psychology, mindset, discipline, habits, and human behavior. Additional insights are drawn from publicly available interviews, speeches, biographies, and educational resources focused on personal growth and self-mastery.

- Clear, James. *Atomic Habits: An Easy & Proven Way to Build Good Habits & Break Bad Ones.* Avery, 2018.
- Dweck, Carol S. *Mindset: The New Psychology of Success.* Random House, 2006.
- Newport, Cal. *Deep Work: Rules for Focused Success in a Distracted World.* Grand Central Publishing, 2016.
- Covey, Stephen R. *The 7 Habits of Highly Effective People.* Free Press, 1989.
- Duhigg, Charles. *The Power of Habit: Why We Do What We Do in Life and Business.* Random House, 2012.
- Frankl, Viktor E. *Man's Search for Meaning.* Beacon Press, 1946.
- McKeown, Greg. *Essentialism: The Disciplined Pursuit of Less.* Crown Business, 2014.

Additional inspiration and educational perspectives were drawn from publicly available interviews, lectures, articles, and biographies of influential thinkers, entrepreneurs, athletes, psychologists, and leaders whose experiences contribute to the understanding of discipline, resilience, mindset, and personal transformation.

About the Author

Asharaf Ali is a mindset-focused writer who is passionate about helping people overcome their inner limitations and discover their true potential. His work centers on a simple but powerful belief: the greatest obstacles in life are often not outside us, but within us.

Through thoughtful insights, reflective questions, and practical exercises, he encourages readers to understand their fears, break destructive patterns, and build the discipline needed to create meaningful change. His writing focuses on clarity, self-awareness, and the courage required to move beyond comfort and into growth.

In **The Mountain Within You,** Asharaf Ali explores how self-sabotage, fear, and limiting beliefs quietly shape our lives—and how anyone can transform those inner struggles into strength. He believes that personal transformation is not about sudden breakthroughs, but about small, intentional actions repeated every day.

His goal is to make personal growth accessible and realistic for everyone, regardless of their background or circumstances. Rather than offering quick fixes or empty motivation, his work emphasizes patience, responsibility, and the power of consistent effort.

Asharaf believes that the journey of self-mastery begins with a simple realization: the mountain standing in your way may actually be the path that leads you to your greatest strength.

Your Journey Begins Now

The mountain within you was never meant to stop you. It was meant to reveal your strength.

Keep growing.

Keep learning.

Keep climbing.

— Asharaf Ali

9 789359 124940

Printed at Repro India Ltd.